ORCAS
High Seas Supermen

by Ellen Hopkins

COVER-TO-COVER BOOKS

Perfection Learning®

About the Author

Ellen Hopkins lives with her family, four dogs, two cats, and three tanks of fish near Carson City, Nevada. A California native, Ellen moved to the Sierra Nevada to ski. While writing for a Lake Tahoe newspaper, she discovered many exciting things and fascinating people.

Dedication and Acknowledgment

This book is dedicated to the selfless people making the world a better place for all animals. With special thanks to Randy Eaton, Craig Webster, and Michael Magaw.

Cover and Book Design: Deborah Lea Bell
Cover Photo: Six Flags Marine World
Inside Illustration: Michael A. Aspengren, Gregory Nemec (p. 64)

Photo Credits: Jeff Foott Productions (www.jfoott.com) pp. 4, 5, 7, 8 (top and bottom), 9, 10, 11, 13, 14, 15, 16, 21, 22, 26, 27, 31, 32, 33, 34, 35, 37, 45, 46, 49 **Oregon Coast Aquarium** p. 55
Six Flags Marine World pp. 1, 40, 41, 42, 44, 47

Image Credits: ArtToday (some images copyright www.arttoday.com) **Corel** pp. 19, 53, 54 **Dover Publications** p. 56

Table of Contents

Introduction

Can We Free Willy?

Have you seen the *Free Willy* movies? In the first one, a boy named Jesse makes friends with Willy, a captive killer whale. When Willy's life is in danger, Jesse sets him free.

Free Willy II follows the orca as he returns to his native waters and finds his **pod**. Are these stories only tall tales? Or could they really happen?

Could an orca and a person become friends and learn to communicate? Could a captured killer whale return to the sea? Could he locate his home and family? If he did, would they remember him? Would he learn the behaviors he'd need to know to survive?

Some scientists don't think so. But a growing number believe it is possible. Right now, the first-ever release of a captured orca is underway. You may have helped. Kids across the country collected pennies for the Keiko Project.

Did you know Keiko played Willy in the movies? After 20 years of captivity, he'd grown tired of living in a little tank. Think how you'd feel locked in a tiny room for 20 years. You'd get bored and want to go somewhere. You'd want to play with your friends and get some exercise. You might even feel a little crazy.

That's what happened to Keiko. He'd outgrown his tank. That made him grouchy. Worse, he was getting sick. The time had come to send him home. He's gone from Mexico to Oregon to a large holding pen in his native Iceland. He's learning to hunt. His temper and health have improved. He awaits release. And the world wants to know, "Can we really free 'Willy'?"

A better question might be, "Should we?"

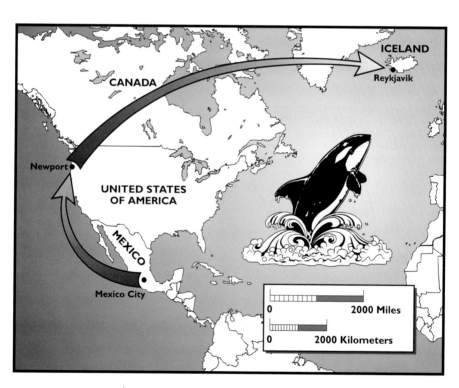

CHAPTER 1

Giant Dolphins

Check out that giant black shadow cruising beneath the whitecaps. It speeds toward shore. Then suddenly it stops. A triangular shape breaks the surface and slowly starts to rise. Up, up, five feet into the air it goes.

Only one thing in the ocean has a **dorsal** fin that tall. With a tremendous *phoot!*, a spray of air and water blasts skyward. As the old whalers' saying goes, "Thar she blows!"

Romans named the creature "orca," after an underworld **ogre**. Its Spanish name means "**assassin**." The Scandinavians know it as "blubber chopper." We call it "killer whale."

Does the orca live up to its bloodthirsty reputation? Is it a ferocious man-eater? Is it all teeth and no brain? Ask anyone who knows them. They'll tell you, "No way!"

Well, then what exactly is an orca? *Orcinus orca* is a **marine** mammal. All mammals bear their young live and nurse them. They breathe air and have hair. Orcas are born with exactly two hairs on their face.

Mammals are warm-blooded. Their body temperature stays the same whether it's hot or cold. Whales stay warm in cold water because their huge bodies and many layers of fat, or *blubber*, hold heat. Blubber works much like the insulation in your house.

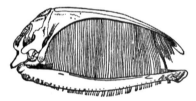

jawbone showing baleens

There are two kinds of whales. Baleen whales have no teeth. Hundreds of thin plates called "baleens" line their mouths. These plates filter **plankton** from seawater.

Orcas are toothed whales (*odontoceti*). Sperm whales, belugas, and dolphins are also toothed whales. In fact, orcas are really dolphins.

That's right, they're a king-sized version of Flipper!

They don't look much alike. Dolphins are gray. A big bottlenose like Flipper might grow to 10 feet in length. Most are half that size.

Male, or bull, orcas can grow 32 feet long and weigh 11 tons. The females, or cows, might reach 28 feet and 8 tons. Yet orca families are **matriarchal**. "Mom" is always in charge. That is, unless something threatens the group. Then the larger bulls take over. They act as bodyguards.

That orca you spotted is a young bull. Let's call him Cal.

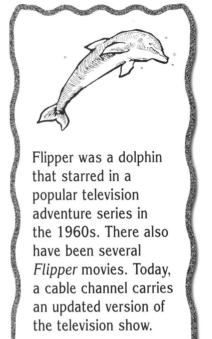

Flipper was a dolphin that starred in a popular television adventure series in the 1960s. There also have been several *Flipper* movies. Today, a cable channel carries an updated version of the television show.

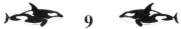

His shiny black back breaks the surface. Then he flips, swimming the sidestroke. Check out his bright white belly and cool polka dots.

If you study Cal closely, you could pick him out of an "orca lineup." Like human fingerprints, an orca's dorsal fin and gray saddle patch behind it are one of a kind. That lets marine scientists track and study individual orcas.

Before 1965, we didn't know much about orcas. They looked scary. Most people put them right up there with sharks.

Fishermen hated them and called them "devilfish." These devilfish feasted on hooked halibut and pulled down nets used to snag herring.

Halibut and herring are high-dollar cash crops in Iceland. But you can't blame the orcas for choosing easy meals.

During the late 1960s and early 1970s, nearly 60 killer whales were taken captive in the Pacific Northwest. Most went off to aquariums. But several died during the captures. That made headlines.

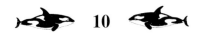

The Canadian government decided to weigh the damage to its British Columbian orcas. Everyone believed there were thousands. But in 1973, Dr. Michael Bigg conducted an orca **census**. He counted only a few hundred. Out of 300, one-fifth of the population—60 of them—was gone.

As Dr. Bigg worked, he noticed every orca had unique markings, nicks, and scars. He photographed each whale and "named" it with a letter of the alphabet plus a number (A1, for instance).

Now most of the world's orcas have an alphanumeric name. Researchers update the photos yearly. They keep track of the whales' travels. The process is called *photo identification*.

Scientists have discovered three types of orcas. They are "resident," "offshore," and "transient." Resident orcas never stray far from their native waters. The mysterious offshore orcas voyage far out to

sea. It's tough to learn more about them. Transients usually travel in small groups of two or three. But larger pods are not uncommon. They travel many miles, following their favored prey.

Killer whales hang out in every ocean in the world. You can find them in tropical waters and the open sea. Most prefer colder water close to land. But they'll go anywhere food is plentiful. They have even been seen in shallow bays and river mouths. In fact, some have been sighted five miles upriver from the ocean.

As the ocean's top **predators**, orcas are *carnivores*, or meat eaters. Orcas are like other successful predators, such as lions, wolves, eagles, and humans. They sit at the top of the food chain. Humans are their only natural enemy.

Orcas catch their prey with interlocking, cone-shaped teeth. But unless the catch is something really big, orcas swallow it whole.

How big is "really" big? Hunting cooperatively as a pack, these 10-ton torpedoes sometimes kill 100-ton blue whales. They break the Antarctic ice pack or create waves to sweep walrus into the sea. They herd schools of fish against the shore. And then the orcas pick them off one by one. Once in a while, orcas jump onto a beach to snatch sea lion snacks. They even leap into the air to catch seabirds in flight!

All marine mammals except manatees risk becoming orca food. Apparently, manatee meat tastes awful. Seafood is more to their liking—fish, whales, stingrays, even sharks. No wonder orcas have a fierce reputation. But they don't kill for fun. They only hunt to eat. And they often share feeding grounds with competitors like porpoises.

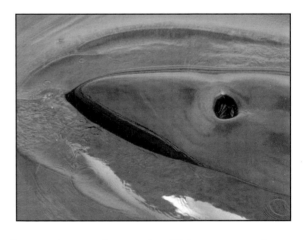

Orcas don't make war. Nor do they fight one another for food, mates, or territory. And they don't eat people at all!

Phoot! There's Cal, spouting again. That's how orcas breathe. Whales aren't fish. They don't have gills, which take air from water. They have lungs and must surface to breathe.

Baleen whales have two nostrils on top of their heads. Toothed whales have only one blowhole. When they inhale, strong muscles open the blowhole wide. Then they snap it tightly shut.

How long can you hold your breath? An orca can hold its breath for almost an hour!

Whales' muscles store oxygen. When they dive, their hearts beat slower. That *conserves*, or saves, oxygen. After a dive, they must take several breaths before going under again. This restores the oxygen their muscles have lost.

The breathing process doesn't just happen. Voluntary breathing takes thought. That's why only half of an orca's brain sleeps at one time. The other half stays alert to control breathing.

Orcas can exhale underwater. See that column of bubbles? If you followed it down to deep water, you'd probably find an orca

letting air out of its lungs. Scientists think that's one way whales find one other.

Now look at Cal. He's *spy-hopping*. He's standing right up on his tail to get a better look at something. Orcas' eyes work well, both in and out of water.

If you open your eyes underwater, everything looks blurry. But an orca's eyes adjust so everything's crystal clear. Orcas also "see" with sonar, or sound waves.

Orcas have excellent hearing. But they have almost no sense of smell.

Whales are really into touch. Orcas, especially, love to rub against things. If they spy a log far out at sea, they'll go brush it. They just want to know how it feels.

Orcas visit "rubbing beaches." There they scratch their backs on sand and stones. Afterward, they often swim slowly through kelp beds. The soft, gooey seaweed soothes their skin. Sometimes, they even take a clump with them, draping it over their heads and backs.

Keep an eye on Cal. He's in a playful mood. You just might see him jump out of the water and then flip upside down in midair.

This is called "breaching."

Orcas breach for fun, just like you do cartwheels and somersaults. Every day, they play and swim as well as hunt. Young females often "baby-sit" so mother orcas can play or hunt. Bulls and grannies also help.

Orcas start having babies between 11 and 15 years of age. A cow carries her calf for 17 months. That's almost twice as long as a person does. At birth, the calves are six to eight feet long. They are fully developed and able to swim. Human babies are pretty helpless. But baby orcas must keep up with their mamas right away.

Calves nurse for about a year. An orca's milk glands are inside her body. So she squirts milk into her baby's mouth. The calf rolls its tongue into a tube, like a straw. Then the calf doesn't lose a drop.

The milk is very rich, and the little orca grows quickly. When the time is right, the milk turns salty so it tastes bad. The calf then learns to hunt.

Since we've only studied orcas for 30 years, no one knows exactly how long they live. But scientists think females in the wild might reach the ripe old age of 90! The average lifespan is

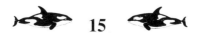

around 50 years. For some reason, the bulls live only half as long. Captive orcas rarely make it past 30 years.

The wild populations have researchers worried. Like other whales, sick orcas often beach themselves. Dr. Randy Eaton has studied wild orcas for 20 years. He says, "They strand themselves so other orcas don't catch whatever it is they've got." Lately, what they've got is toxic levels of poisons like PCB, DDE, and mercury.

Craig Webster has been interested in orcas since the late 1960s. That was when many of the killer whales were captured in the Pacific Northwest. "I didn't know why then," he said. "But I felt it was the wrong thing to do to such a magnificent animal."

Together with John Ford, president of the Northwest Killer Whale Alliance (NKWA), Craig has studied Pacific Coast killer whales since the late 1980s. He believes environmental problems threaten the entire ocean world.

"The toothed cetaceans of the Pacific Northwest are in extreme danger from toxins. In what seems like a [clean] part of the ocean, mercury in the top predator has risen to shocking levels. This is a problem for all of us. Remember, another top predator in this world is man."

The orcas, it seems, are giving us fair warning.

CHƏPTER

Settlers and Wanderers

Once upon a time, whales were land mammals. They roamed prehistoric Europe, Africa, and North America. But these ancestors looked nothing like whales.

Fossils suggest cetaceans' earliest relatives were the land-dwelling mesonyx. Although they resembled wolves, mesonyx had hooves. This points to a weird fact. Whales are closely related to cattle!

Other evidence bears this out. Like all **ruminants**, both cows

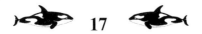

and whales have many stomachs. These digest food in stages.

Their sleep patterns are similar too. Both are active day and night. They only nap from time to time.

Then whales moved into the sea. Their features changed. Front legs became flippers, which they used to steer and balance. The skeleton inside a flipper looks a lot like a human arm and hand. It even has five fingers. All that's left of the hind legs are two hipbones.

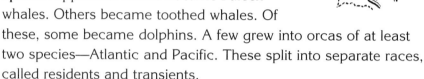

As these animals **evolved**, different **species** appeared. Some became baleen whales. Others became toothed whales. Of these, some became dolphins. A few grew into orcas of at least two species—Atlantic and Pacific. These split into separate races, called residents and transients.

Although they share the same waters, the two races differ in many ways. Scientists don't know what caused this split. But they think it happened over 100,000 years ago.

Offshore orcas have only recently been discovered. No one knows if they are a unique race or simply another community.

Since the early 1990s, more than 200 offshores have been identified. But scientists are clueless about their diet, travel range, and other habits. Craig Webster and the NKWA have set their sights on learning more.

Transients and residents look a little different. A transient's dorsal fin is a bit more pointed and its saddle patch sits farther forward. But the real difference between the two is the way they live and feed.

Residents eat only fish and stay close to home. Transients cruise long distances. They hunt other marine mammals. They don't eat fish at all.

Resident populations live off Iceland and Norway and in the coastal waters of British Columbia and Washington State. The

Pacific groups have been studied the most because in the summer they only eat salmon. That makes them easy to watch during salmon season.

Orcas are social animals. They like company and rarely travel alone.

A mother orca and her children stay together for life. Her sons may leave for short periods to mate with cows from other pods. But they always come back to "Mom." This is a maternal group.

Likewise, when her daughters have their own calves, they may separate a little to take care of their kids. But "Granny" will always be nearby. This is a subpod.

Resident societies look like this.

Maternal Group
mother and children

Subpod
mother, daughter, and her grandchildren

Pod
extended family

Clan
pods that "speak" the same way

Community
pods that live and travel together, like a moving town

Imagine a big family. Brothers, sisters, parents, grandparents, aunts, uncles, and cousins all living together. That is what resident orcas do. These pods may have up to 50 members.

All orcas "speak" the same language. This odd assortment of clicks, calls, and whistles carries great distances, both over and under the water.

But different pods have distinct **dialects**. It's like Americans. Most speak English. But Texans don't sound the same as people in Wisconsin. Their dialects differ. But they understand each other.

Icelandic orcas sound a little different from those in the Pacific. Both groups have various ways of speaking. Pods that share a dialect belong to the same clan.

British Columbia

Queen Charlotte Strait

Cape Scott

Cape Cook

Vancouver Island

Campbell River

Vancouver

Pacific Ocean

Haro Strait

Northern Resident Community

Southern Resident Community

Puget Sound

Seattle

Washington

Communities are orcas that usually hang out together. In Washington State and British Columbia, resident pods form two communities— southern and northern. The northern community has about 200 orcas in 16 pods. The southern group consists of 100 members in 3 pods.

The communities are close to each other. But they rarely mix. Scientists don't know why.

Resident pods often "rest" close together. They swim slowly and breathe in **unison**. Breathing together seems to help them keep track of one another, even when half asleep. Orcas also lie on the surface, not moving at all.

Usually the entire subpod "snoozes" quietly together. These naps may last a few minutes or go on for hours. One guard stays awake. It keeps watch. After a while, it sounds a "wake-up" call.

Then it's time to move on.

Orca pods travel in tight formation. They all go the same direction at 3 to 12 **knots**. Residents don't cover the miles transients do. But they do move from place to place.

Upon arrival, a pod calls out a loud "we're here." Other orcas answer. And boy, does it get noisy!

Orcas love to "party." They spend many hours mingling with other pods, even those from different clans.

When a new group arrives, a "welcome party" goes to meet it. Imagine pods, 20 orcas in each, swimming slowly toward each other in two tight lines. Some 30 feet apart, they stop and rest for several seconds.

Finally, the fun begins. The groups join. Brushing and rubbing against each other, they say hello as only orcas do. The greeting party then turns around. It swims ahead of the new arrivals.

The northern residents often escort the newcomers to the Johnstone Strait rubbing beaches. These beaches are covered with flat, smooth stones. The orcas dive, exhale hard, and throw themselves onto the shore. Then they flip, flop, and wiggle. They rub their bodies over the stones.

Several may use the beach at once. Or they line up and wait just offshore for their turn. More than fun, this helps them shed skin. So does swimming, diving, breaching, brushing, and rubbing. Orcas replace their skin from 3 to 7 times a day.

There's Cal. He sure looks hungry! It takes a lot of fish to satisfy an orca. It can eat up to 5 percent of its body weight every day. That could be up to 1,100 pounds of food!

Cal's pod joins three others. They're ready to hunt. Their target is salmon.

The orcas spread out until they're 150 feet apart. The line advances slowly. The orcas are clicking and whistling constantly. Honk! Salmon spotted!

Cal and the others close in. They herd the fish toward shore. They trap the salmon against the rocks and then snatch them one by one.

Suddenly, the whales back off. They dive, swim to a new location, and start all over again. They won't wipe out entire schools. They seem to know that salmon must spawn or there won't be more next year.

Orca hunts vary, depending on the fish. The whales dive deep for sockeye salmon. These fish swim in cooler depths.

Chum salmon school near the surface. They often get caught in strong riptides. Orca pods shallow-dive those currents for hours at a time looking for chum salmon.

The big Chinook salmon like to hide in rocky crevices. An orca will patiently work those cracks to flush out the fish.

In Norway and Iceland, residents chase herring into a tight ball. Then they stun the fish with their tail flukes. It's time for the feast.

Transient orcas would never elbow in on a resident hunt. In fact, they steer clear of those noisy residents. All that clicking and whistling!

That's no way to catch a sea lion, walrus, or whale. Marine mammals rarely go down without a fight. A sea lion bite or scratch can turn deadly if infection sets in. So transients hunt quietly on the sly. But their efforts are also highly coordinated.

Scientists aren't sure how transients travel. They might move in small groups and then gather to hunt. Or they might cruise in large pods, spreading out when they reach a certain area. Either way, transients have developed skills residents don't need.

They can change their blows and sonar to confuse prey. Sometimes they breach on top of their prey and knock it out. They've even been spotted cruising behind a noisy **ferry**. They were using it as cover to sneak up on porpoises.

When hunting dolphins, orcas surround a large group. Then they slowly close in. As the circle tightens, the prey swims round and round inside it. Suddenly, three or four hunters enter the ring and choose victims. When they're done, others take their turn. Larger whales go down in similar fashion. That includes the blue whale, the largest animal on earth!

Transients are opportunistic. They'll take what they can find. The "LA Pod" cruises the West Coast from Baja to Monterey. It stops frequently near Los Angeles. The pod's 15 members seem to break all the rules, especially CA2.

CA2 is a 28-year-old female with a craving for shark. Videotape caught the 20-foot orca attacking a 10-foot great white shark! She and her LA Pod are the only killer whales known to attack and eat large sharks. Maybe they don't like the competition. Maybe they're keeping Southern California's coastal waters safe from man-eaters. Or maybe they just like the taste.

Most transients prefer **pinnipeds**, such as seals, walrus, and the like. These orcas travel thousands of coastline miles hunting the pinnipeds.

Orcas use a number of techniques, including breaking ice floes, creating waves, beaching themselves, and striking their victims with their tails. They'll do whatever it takes to capture prey.

In 1997, scientists in Alaska noticed something strange. Sea otters were disappearing! In one 500-mile stretch, their numbers dropped from over 50,000 to less than 6,000.

After months of observation, there was only one answer—orcas! But why? Otters weren't the whales' favorite food. In decades of study, the researchers had never seen them eat one!

The scientists came up with a theory. Too many nutritious fish, like perch and herring, were being caught by fishermen. Fewer fish meant fewer pinnipeds. So the orcas turned to the next best thing—sea otters.

Is that bad? You bet. Besides being really cute, otters are an important link in the coastal food chain. Less of them means too many sea urchins. These creatures eat kelp and are well on their way to destroying the coastal Alaskan kelp beds. That will affect many animals, from barnacles to bald eagles.

Craig Webster commented, "It's obvious that overfishing affects a fish-eating predator. But it might affect transient orcas even more. Less fish in our northern waters means less pinnipeds. That means the whales are also in trouble."

Could people be in trouble next?

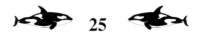

CHAPTER

High Seas Supermen

What's faster than a speeding motorboat? Able to leap tall breakers in a single breach? Is it a bird? Is it a plane? Is it a flying octopus? No. It's Cal, the high seas superman!

What, exactly, makes him Superman? Well, he's a speed

demon. Cal can swim at 32 knots. That's pretty fast for an animal that weighs 10 tons.

And he's strong. Using his tail flukes, Cal can push himself out of the water and into the air. That's sort of like bench-pressing 20,000 pounds.

Whales are very smart. Compare the size of Cal's brain to his body. He's on the same curve as people. In fact, he's one of the few animals with a brain larger than a human's. After years of study, scientists know these creatures rely on more than **instinct**. Orcas, like dolphins, learn quickly and can **reason**.

Researcher John Lilly used a classic training tool on a dolphin. Each time it made a right choice, the dolphin got a fish. This is called "positive reinforcement." Reward rather than punishment promotes learning, or making more right choices. The dolphin mastered several tests and collected his reward.

Later, an assistant found a pile of fish at the other end of the pool. The dolphin hadn't eaten any! John realized the dolphin had been reinforcing John's behavior. The dolphin was smart enough to know why the man was giving him fish. So the dolphin "rewarded" the man by doing the task. And the man performed by giving the dolphin a fish. In other words, the dolphin was training the man!

Whale brains even have built-in maps and calendars.

Australian whalers tell this story.

Every year for over a century, on the exact same day, orcas gathered outside Sydney Harbor. The whaling boats followed them to the yearly gray whale migration. The orcas drove the gray whales toward the harpooners. The men took their limit. Then they rewarded the orcas. They tossed back the orcas' favorite parts, the tongues and lips, for them to eat.

Okay, orcas are fast, strong, and smart. But what really makes Cal like Superman is his "X-ray vision." No joke. Eyes rely on light to see. Deep down where sunlight can't reach, eyes are pretty useless. Yet orcas not only "see," they see in 3-D! They do it with sonar, or sound waves.

Whales use sound and hearing like land animals use vision and smell. Orcas vocalize in three ways. They use whistles, calls, and clicks. All are made by air moving in and out of their nasal sacs. Whistles communicate information over short distances. Calls can be as loud as jet engines and carry for many miles. Both sounds keep pod members in touch with one another at all times.

Orca calls are signals which "beat" in a certain pattern. Each clan has its own collection of calls. They are shared by one or more pods. Dr. John Ford dubbed these language patterns "dialects." Researchers use photo identification to recognize orcas by sight. Dialects let them identify groups at night or from a distance.

Clicks are part of their sonar system. Bats use **echolocation** to fly night skies. Shrews use it to catch insects and mice in the dark. Whales use sonar to explore their dark watery world.

Deep in its head, an orca's nasal sacs are located behind the **melon**. The melon is an organ that acts like a lens. It focuses the sound into a narrow beam. Think of the laserlike ray Superman shoots from his eyes. When the sound wave strikes an object, some of its energy bounces back. It's like an echo.

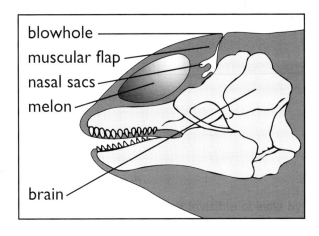

Orcas don't have outer ears. They "hear" with their lower jaw. It picks up the echo and transmits it to the middle ear. Once the echo is received, the orca clicks again. The time lapse between click and echo tells it how far away the object is. The strength of the signal shows direction. If it's stronger on the left jaw, the orca goes left. By constantly clicking, it can track objects and home in on them.

Click, click, click. Big, fat salmon, 20 yards south. Click, click. Closing in. Click. Got him!

It all happens very quickly. Sound moves four times faster in water than air. Factor in an orca's underwater speed. That fish doesn't have a chance!

Orcas, like dolphins, continue to amaze the people who study them. One researcher showed a dolphin some hollow balls. On the outside, they looked exactly the same. But the hollow center of each was a tiny bit different in size. Using sonar, the dolphin could tell the difference. Think of Superman "seeing" deep into a building. How did the dolphin do it?

The dolphin echolocated the balls. Some of the sonar bounced off of them. The rest penetrated the balls. The sound wave went inside the balls. It "saw" how big the centers were.

Then it echoed that information. Dolphins "see" inside things through sound, just like Superman does with his X-ray vision.

Pretend you can see inside someone. What do you know about that person? You can see muscles. Are they weak or strong? You can see lungs and kidneys. Are they sick or healthy? You can see the heart beat. Is it fast or slow? Is the person afraid?

Randy Eaton said that's one reason orcas don't fight with one another. "They already know which ones are stronger. They have nothing to prove."

In another study, a dolphin in one tank mastered a test after several tries. Then he passed the test answer to his buddy in the connecting tank. Tall walls blocked the second dolphin's view. His eyes couldn't see the experiment. Yet he aced the test on the first try. ESP? No, not extrasensory perception. SSP—sonic-sensory perception. The first dolphin told the second one what to do using sonar.

A new theory called "big bang" suggests that orcas kill or stun their prey with bursts of sound. When hunting salmon, orcas make loud, pulsing noises like drumbeats. When recorded and played back, these sounds killed or stunned other fish.

The big-bang theory could explain

• how dolphins catch prey that should easily outswim them

• why they've lost a large number of teeth from their once-powerful jaws

• why they don't fight with one another. If they can "death ray" prey, they can death ray one another!

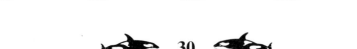

If sonar can injure, could it also heal? Maybe! Studies conducted since 1971 show swimming with dolphins can help people with Down's syndrome, autism, depression, ADHD (attention deficit hypertensive disorder), and spinal cord injuries. Mentally retarded children greatly improved their learning skills after dipping with dolphins!

Sonar also seems to boost the production of infection-fighting T cells. Some say swimming with dolphins makes people relax. This aids the immune system. But David Cole, a young computer scientist, said relaxation can't explain the changes in brain waves and blood chemistry. He thinks those changes are caused by echolocation.

An orca's sonar creates an incredible amount of energy. There is certainly enough to move molecules around. Maybe enough to rip them apart. That could change lots of things, including a person's blood or brain. If science could copy that process, think of the good it might do!

Orcas really do have a lot to teach us.

The Orca-Human Connection

Your four-man dinghy zips across the bay. Several hundred yards out, you stop the motor and shout, "Cal! Cal!" Nearby, you hear his whistles.

In minutes, a dozen orcas surround your boat. A cow nudges its calf your way. The little bull spy-hops. It looks you right in the eye. "Hello" it calls in some resident orca dialect. Hey, it could happen!

Randy Eaton fell for orcas in 1979. As an animal-behavior specialist, he'd studied everything from lions to belugas. He found them all interesting. But the big orcas captivated him. Every summer, Randy and his Orca Project volunteers observed the Pacific Northwestern pods. Early on, they wondered how best to make friends with them. A young cow showed them the way.

"The first time she heard me call 'Nicola' out loud," Randy remembered, "she came toward the boat." Apparently, she liked the name enough to keep it. Every time Randy called "Nicola," she swam toward his boat.

Later, he and his friends stood on shore. Spotting the friendly orca, they invited, "Nicola! Nicola! Come here and see us."

She stopped, turned toward them, and summoned her pod. The females gathered their calves. This greeting party watched the people watching them.

"Then two at a time," said Randy, "the cows swam toward us with a calf. The baby spy-hopped over and over. When he'd had

a good look, he returned to his pod so another could take a turn. One by one, every calf studied us up close."

Randy believes Nicola and the others introduced their babies to a pod of friendly humans. He called it "a meeting of nations, a true exchange between species, and the high point of ten years of fieldwork. So far the best way to attract, befriend, and communicate with wild orcas is simply to call them."

Wild orcas want to be friends with people. If that sounds strange, it should.

How many wild lions, wolves, or eagles make friends with humans? Remember, humans are their only natural enemy. Wolves run. Eagles fly. Lions attack. They even eat people.

An orca could easily swallow a person whole. At the very least, it could drown a person or inflict a world of hurt. Instead, these gentle giants swim peacefully beside us.

Every summer on Puget Sound, hundreds of whale watchers boat and float among wild orca pods. Picture floating in an inner tube next to and over school bus-sized dolphins. Some people do. Others get right in the water and swim with them. Most

prefer to stay on one of the 60 or so commercial whale-watching boats. Figure in motorboats, sailboats, kayaks, and rafts, and that's a lot of people. And all of them want to get close to orcas.

San Juan Island residents complain that you can't see the whales for the boats. They say boaters upset the orcas. They zig too close and zag too fast between them. So far, so lucky. No accidents have been recorded. But is it only a matter of time?

"Whale watching has likely dangers," explained Craig Webster. "People have to remember they aren't in a marine park. The orcas aren't there to perform. There's a chance they won't even show. If they do, it's on their own schedule."

Craig said problems pop up when whale-watching operators try too hard to give their customers thrills. "Most are wonderful people who have the best interests of the whales in mind. Those who take the time to understand these animals give people a show unlike anything they've ever seen. Orcas, living their everyday lives, are more amazing than any marine park act."

And what do the orcas think? How many people are too many?

Researcher Bob Otis went to San Juan in 1990. His mission was to prove the boats bothered the orcas. For seven years, he watched more and more people arrive.

The U.S. guidelines state that people should stay 100 yards away. But they pushed closer and closer to the whales. In the end, Bob reached a surprising conclusion. The orcas accept the situation!

Have they ever felt differently? The North Pacific peoples all have similar legends.

Once, my father's mother's brother attacked a blackfish. The orca had no choice. It fought back and won. It found no joy in victory, for it has never harmed another human. Among our nations, there's been peace ever since.

The ancestor might differ. But the theme is the same. Orcas attack only in **revenge** and only if the person assaulted them first.

Written history tells another story. There isn't one recorded instance of an orca attacking a person. Not even in self-defense.

Orcas are bigger, stronger, and probably just as smart. Why don't they try to hurt the only species that hurts them? Scientists aren't sure. Some think the whales realize people could wipe them out. So why give them reason to?

They aren't exactly afraid of us. As the ocean's top predator, orcas have no fear of anything in their environment.

When not threatened, they are extremely curious. They want to know more about things they don't understand. "Maybe that's why they don't fight the capture nets," guessed Randy Eaton. "They want to learn from us. And they want to teach us."

One onlooker called an orca capture the most dramatic thing he'd ever witnessed.

Orcas are chased toward bays or inlets. Once inside, a net is stretched across the opening to cut off escape. The victims are usually young. Luckier pod members return to open water.

Think of the whistling and calling! Imagine if someone

kidnapped you. Wouldn't you be scared? Wouldn't you scream? Wouldn't your family call out for help or try to stop the kidnapper?

Yet the orcas do not attack their captors. Swimmers guide them into transport slings, using only their hands. Though frightened, most orcas go willingly. The ones that don't, let the air out of their lungs. Then they sink and drown. Rather than hurt someone, they resort to suicide!

The first successful capture was actually an accident. On a summer morning in 1965, Alaskan fisherman Bill Lechkobit checked his nets near the salmon cannery at Namu. He found more than salmon trapped inside. He'd netted an orca bull calf.

Almost 400 miles away, Seattle Aquarium owner Ted Griffin heard the news. An orca! Nobody had an orca! If he could find a way to transport the bull, he'd have a real crowd pleaser.

Griffin's team invented a floating pen for the tough 375-mile trip. The weather gods smiled. The orca made it. Namu moved into a big concrete tank on the Seattle waterfront.

Griffin knew his stuff. Namu was an instant hit. Everyone

wanted to see him. And as people learned about him, they began to understand him. He wasn't a vicious predator. He was a smart, sensitive, even funny, creature.

Namu trained easily and established a deep relationship with his handlers. Were all orcas like that? The first captive killer whale made people want to know.

Eleven months later, Namu's pod came looking for him. For several days, they swam in Puget Sound, calling in his familiar dialect. Though he was treated well at the aquarium, Namu missed his family. He tried to jump out of his tank to reunite with them. He died trying.

After that, every aquarium wanted an orca and was willing to pay the price. The captures began. Before 1976, the Pacific coast pods took the hardest hit. Sixty orcas, nearly 20 percent of the population, were taken or died in those attempts.

Then the state of Washington took Sea World to court. The settlement ended captures in the Pacific Northwest.

Capture teams moved on to Iceland. They continued there until 1989. Since then, six orcas have been taken—one in Argentina and five in Japan. The 1997 Japanese captures caused a global outcry. By then, most of the world had outlawed catching or killing whales. But Japan has never seen eye to eye on the issue. They used a loophole in the whaling treaties. They claimed the orcas were captured for "scientific study." Two of the five died. The others now perform in Japanese marine parks.

Between 1965 and 1997, 134 orcas were taken into captivity. Most were residents between two and six years of age. All but two went to aquariums. Ishmael and Ahab joined the U.S. Navy's Project Deep Ops.

These two were rounded up with 65 others in 1968, near Yukon Harbor, WA. All but five young bulls were released.

Ishmael and Ahab went to Hawaii. In February 1971, two years and four months after his capture, Ishmael escaped off Oahu. Ahab stayed with the Navy until he died in 1974. Cuddles went to England, where he died in April 1974. Two months later, Mamuk died at Sea-Arama Marine World in Galveston, TX. Haida went to Sealand Victoria. He died there in 1982.

Ishmael's fate remains a mystery. The other four died before they were 15. Wild orcas may live to be 90. But captive orcas rarely make it to the age of 30. Aquarium people say it's because of lung infections and pneumonia. Animal rights people say it's boredom.

Of the 134 captured orcas, only 30 are alive today. Of the 60 Pacific Northwesterners, only Sea World's Corky and Lolita at the Miami Seaquarium have survived.

At 33, Lolita is the oldest in captivity. Yes, she's healthy. But it's safe to say she'd live longer in the wild.

A move is underway to return Lolita to her pod. It still swims off Puget Sound. The Tokitae Foundation wants to bring her back to Washington State. The Miami Seaquarium says "no way."

The question is, "What's best for Lolita?" She's safe in Florida. Is she happy there? Or does she long to swim again in Puget Sound?

The Tokitae Foundation is a nonprofit group. Its goals are to inform and communicate with the public about whales and dolphins. The immediate concern of the group is the Lolita Come Home Project. Find out more about Lolita and the project at www.freelolita.net/tok.html

Star Performers

In Vallejo, California, on a sunny afternoon, 3,500 people file into the Whale Stadium. Grown-ups find shady seats. But kids jam the front rows. They giggle at the underwater phantom circling the tank. Each of them wonders, "Will I get wet?" Not wet. Drenched!

"Welcome to Six Flags/Marine World," begins the announcer. "I know you're all anxious to meet the star of our show. In Scandinavian, her name means 'Little Sweetheart.' At 6,000 pounds, she isn't so little. But she definitely is a sweetheart. Ladies and gentlemen, all eyes down front. This is Vigga!"

The orca throws herself out of the water onto a ledge, flips her tail, and gives the crowd a toothy grin. A trainer rewards her with a fish and toots a little whistle. Vigga slides back into the water. She's ready for her next trick or behavior. Some are just plain fun, like breaching to get the audience wet. Others are awesome, like leaping straight up to touch a ball 20 feet in the air. The crowd cheers for every one. Vigga enjoys their cheers. It's hard to tell who's having more fun.

Michael Magaw heads Marine World's marine-mammal training program. He has trained exotic animals for 18 years. Eight of those he's devoted to dolphins, orcas, and other sea critters. His love for them clearly shows. "They're like my kids," he said.

Vigga and Michael have been a team for five years. They're more than pals. Michael trusts her "more than most people. I have to. And it's mutual. Vigga trusts me too. It's a give-and-take thing."

Critics would argue that it's not surprising. Orcas need contact. They crave companionship. If they can't get that with their own kind, of course they'll turn to people. Others say making animals do tricks for money is abuse.

Vigga doesn't act abused. And *making* her do tricks? Not likely! At 3 tons, she is roughly 30 times Michael's size. He couldn't make her do much.

Vigga performs two daily shows when the park is open. To her, they are play sessions. In the wild, orcas breach and **porpoise** for fun. The fish reward is icing on the cake. Anchovy icing!

Marine parks do make money. How else could they stay in business? Most businesses have expenses. The cost of keeping marine animals, especially orcas, is pretty steep. There are the fish and the people to feed it to the animals. There's the vet bill. Marine World's animals get complete checkups every three months. The animals are so used to them, they offer their tails so the vet can draw blood. Yes, Vigga too. That's lucky for the vet, who weighs about 5,820 pounds less than the patient!

Keeping a small aquarium at home is a big job. Maintaining an orca tank is a huge task! The water is just like seawater. Keeping it that way means filtering, checking **pH**, adding chemicals, and adjusting the temperature. That's all day, every day.

American marine parks are strictly regulated, by both the

U.S. Department of Agriculture and the Department of Fisheries. Marine World's animals are among the most protected on Earth.

Six trainers work under Michael. At least one of them is usually at the park. Someone is even there in the winter when the park is closed. Sometimes a trainer sleeps there. The job isn't a nice, neat 9-to-5 job. And there are no holidays and

Please DO NOT KNOCK on our window.

weekends off. That's when people visit! "You don't punch a time clock, go home, and forget about work," explained Michael. "It's a way of life."

It's also more than playing with orcas. There are a lot of hard, dirty chores. Everything the trainers use is sterilized twice a day. That includes all the sinks, buckets, floors, and walls. Michael joked, "We all have dishpan hands." They also smell kind of fishy. So would you, if you sorted and fed 300 pounds of fish every day.

Yes, Vigga and the Marine World dolphins are attached to their humans. "We spoil them rotten," promised Michael. In fact, if animals and trainers don't bond, he won't let them work together.

Training an orca takes more than skill and fish treats. It takes communication and mutual respect. A new trainer spends three to six months just getting to know Vigga. Besides learning her body language, the newcomer must earn the orca's trust. Building that relationship is the biggest part of the job.

So how do you train an orca? The behaviors come naturally. The trick is getting them to perform on cue. Trainers do this by reinforcing the natural behaviors. That's where the fresh fish come in.

There are no punishments. Just try to make an orca stand in the corner! Besides, that would break down the trust they've worked so hard to build. If for some reason Vigga is in a bad mood, the trainers go away. They try again later.

Yes, orcas have moods. How can you tell? Think about your own family. Can you tell if your mom is mad by the way she looks at you? Can you tell if your dad is happy by the way he walks through the door? Can you tell if your little sister is excited by the way she talks 100 miles a minute? Same thing goes for the people who know Vigga well.

Vigga has favorite behaviors. Some of them she made up herself! The trainers do what they call "**innovative** sessions." They have a signal which means "go do something," or make something up. "Vigga will go off and squirt or spin or act goofy or stick her tongue out," said Michael. "Then we scan or reinforce that behavior."

It's like when you get a good report card. Your parents make a big deal about it. Maybe they reward you with something you

want. If they do, you'll probably try to get another good report card. And if they reward you again, you'll try harder still.

Orcas learn simple commands in a couple of weeks. They can learn a whole show within six months.

Training mishaps have been few. One trainer drowned. Another was hurt when an orca accidentally breached on top of him. Caution is always the name of the game.

Some orcas seem to dislike unfamiliar people or other marine animals—at least until they get to know them. They may ram a new whale or keep drenching a new trainer standing poolside.

Scientists warn against attaching human feelings to animals. But trainers see all emotions. "If we went outside," said Michael, "and sat next to Vigga's tank, she'd probably come up and splash us. She'd do that to draw my attention away from you to her." Vigga gets jealous!

Can she act funny? Yes. According to Michael, "If we have a stadium full of kids, Vigga will go out there and get them wet just to watch them react. That's pretty funny." Who knew orcas had a sense of humor?

"If the audience is mostly adults, Vigga will get them wet, but

she won't put as much energy into it." Who knew orcas could tell the difference between kids and adults?

"Vigga likes how kids scream and holler and jump around." Who knew orcas watched the audiences watching them?

We might never have known any of those things if we hadn't brought orcas into captivity.

It's a lot harder to study them in the wild. For one thing, wild whales spend a lot of time underwater. When they surface, it's usually for minutes at a time.

Even residents travel. You can't be sure where they'll pop up next. From January through April, they go someplace to "winter." No one knows exactly where. Researchers see, as Michael calls it, "**snippets** of their lives."

Most of what we know about orcas we've learned from those in captivity. We realized how very special they are. So we wanted to keep them safe. Only then did we demand the orca captures stop. Only then did we hold tuna fishermen responsible for killing dolphins. Those things alone, say aquarium people, make captivity worthwhile.

"When I first got into this business, people asked me why I wanted to train fish." Michael laughed. "They didn't even know that dolphins are mammals. It seems amazing now. But they didn't care. Even in this country, we used to kill whales and dolphins. Then *Flipper* came out, and people saw that they're kind of cool. When they fell in love with them, everything changed."

Orcas, Michael pointed out, had the same reputation as great white sharks. They were thought of as mindless killers. They deserved to die. As recently as 1959, the British Columbian government put a machine gun at the entrance to Johnstone Strait to shoot the whales. Happily, they never used it. But the U.S. military has shot "devilfish," as some used to call them.

Now some 30 million people visit marine-life parks every year. Most want to see belugas, orcas, and other dolphins up close and personal. The Vancouver Aquarium alone gets 800,000 visitors yearly. If that many people hit Puget Sound, the resident orcas just might look for a new place to live.

Many aquariums have captive-breeding programs. The earliest weren't very successful. Over half the orcas born in captivity have died. Craig Webster believes that's because they bred different races, creating a strange, new species. With greater care, that situation has improved.

Captive-bred orcas should probably stay in captivity. They've never known any other life. It's doubtful they could survive in the wild.

Aquariums also serve as care centers for stranded, sick, or injured sea mammals. Trainers donate countless hours to helping these creatures get well and return to the ocean. That makes them "good guys."

There really aren't many bad guys. Trainers. Researchers. Environmentalists. Aquarium owners. Aquarium visitors. Whale watchers. All of them love these amazing animals.

Chapter 6

Going Home

Vigga, Lolita, and their captive kin seem healthy. They have bonded deeply with their human friends. They enjoy applause and love to perform. But what happens after the show? How do they feel when the crowds go home and their trainers are busy elsewhere? Do they ever get lonely or long to swim free?

Aquarium personnel say "no way." According to the Miami Seaquarium

- Lolita is healthy and content. Her tank is big enough. Between her trainers and the dolphins in the next tank, she has lots of company.
- There's no scientific reason to release her when she's doing so well.
- After 26 years in captivity, she's conditioned to trust and respond to people, not orcas. That could be her "kiss of death" in the wild.
- There's no guarantee her pod would accept her, even if it could be found.
- Having been in captivity for such a long time, she has forgotten the behaviors she'd need to know to survive in the wild.

Animal rights groups have different answers.

According to the Tokitae Foundation

- Orcas are the most tightly bonded social mammals known. Lolita needs her natural waters and the company of her family. Normal travel takes orcas 75 to 100 miles each day. No way can she do that in an aquarium pool.
- She may tend to trust humans, but she just might prefer her mother and other close family. Her "kiss of death" is captivity.
- Lolita's southern resident pod has been photo identified. Most are still alive. Her mother is among them. She will recognize her daughter and gratefully accept her back.
- Lolita was at least six when captured. So she has a good knowledge of necessary skills. Retiring in her home waters gives her the chance for a long, satisfying life.

The only way to know if a release will work is to try one. That makes the Keiko experiment very important. Follow his story. Then you decide. Should captured orcas go home?

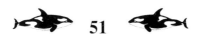

Keiko was born in 1977 or 1978 in Iceland's chilly waters. His pod often followed fishing boats. They gobbled the leftovers tossed overboard. That made them easy targets for the capture nets. In 1979, an Icelandic aquarium offered a large reward for a young orca. Keiko lost his freedom.

Three years later, he went to Marineland Canada. The marine park often trained young orcas for later sale. Keiko moved into a tank with five older orcas. The "new kid" got picked on. He became shy and hard to train. But he was certainly no less valuable. In 1985, a park in Mexico City bought Keiko for $350,000.

At Reino Aventura, Keiko shared a tank with two dolphins. His trainers loved him. And boy, did he attract crowds. A killer whale in the middle of Mexico? Better than must-see TV!

Few realized his 16-foot-deep tank was way too small. Keiko couldn't even get his 20-foot-long body vertical. No more spyhopping. The water was too warm and full of chlorine. Keiko developed a virus that caused sores on his fins and tail flukes. His dorsal fin flopped. Keiko was the star attraction. But he had started to fade.

His life took an odd turn in 1992. Warner Brothers was making a movie called *Free Willy*. They needed a lone orca living in a basic tank with a holding tank they could use. Keiko filled the bill.

As filming progressed, the producers realized that he was in trouble. But they weren't sure how to help him.

Free Willy hit the box office with a bang. People fell for Willy. They wanted to know about Keiko. If he had problems, they wanted them fixed.

Soon, the public demanded, "Free Willy!" Those in the know, however, understood that that was not as easy as it sounded. Still, they looked for a way.

The Free Willy-Keiko Foundation (FWKF) was born. Reino Aventura donated their major attraction. They loved him too.

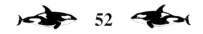

And they didn't want him to die.

Blood tests had shown his immune system failing. He needed a place to **rehabilitate**. And he needed it quickly. There was one big requirement. He needed cooler water near the sea.

The Oregon Coast Aquarium (OCA) fit that description. The OCA specializes in rehabilitation and release.

Keiko's days as a performer ended. But it would take 11 months to build his new home. During that year, he got sicker and sicker. It became a life-and-death situation.

Keiko's journey began in January 1996. The United Parcel Service lent a plane for his adventure. Huge crowds waited outside Reino Aventura. They wanted to say good-bye to the star.

When Keiko landed in Oregon, people lined the streets. They chanted his name in welcome. For the first time in 17 years, Keiko swam in a seawater-filled holding pen. And it was right on the ocean.

It worked wonders. Two years later, the virus had disappeared. His immune system was strong. He could breach and spy-hop. Vertical again! He even began to talk. This is something few captive orcas do. Trainers taught him new tricks like picking out shapes. The exercises made him reason again. That's a must in the wild.

In March 1999, the Free Willy-Keiko Foundation and the Jean-Michel Cousteau Institute became one. These two nonprofit organizations are now Ocean Futures Society. Their mission is to serve as a "voice for the oceans." Keiko is the symbol of the organization. Daily updates on Keiko and information about orcas and other ocean life can be found at www.oceanfutures.com.

In 1998, Keiko's vets declared him healthy. Iceland rolled out the welcome mat. They built a sea pen in a large, deep bay. It was on the migration route of local orca pods. On September 9, Keiko began his journey to his distant home. Thousands of people watched on TV and live Internet feeds. What a show!

Imagine flying a five-ton orca from Oregon to Iceland. It took a really big plane! A chartered 747, in fact. And you can't stop for gas. A whale can only stay in a "bathtub" of water and ice for so long.

Then there was the problem of landing with 10,000 pounds on board. When Keiko's plane touched down on tiny Westman Island, its landing gear broke from the stress. It took a week and nearly one million dollars to fix the damage. But Keiko was home.

He's still in his sea pen. He's learning to hunt live salmon. And he's acting more like a wild orca.

He spends most of his time exploring deep underwater. He's starting to talk to the orcas swimming nearby. Are they waiting for him to join them? Is he anxious to join them?

The FWKF will release him if they feel he's ready. If not, they'll keep him there, near his family, for the rest of his life.

Right now, they're trying to make him less dependent on people.

Some insist a release won't work. Others say it will. Most believe we have to try.

Craig Webster summed it up. "These animals deserve to swim free in their native waters. Keiko may die in this attempt. That is life in the wild. Some live. Some die. But the chance to live free is worth the risk."

Do you agree? What conclusions have you drawn? Could an orca and a person become friends and learn to communicate? Of course. Could a captured orca return to the sea and locate his home and family? Probably. Would his pod remember him? Would you remember your long-lost brother or sister? Could he learn the behaviors he'd need to know to survive? Right now, only Keiko can give us that answer.

So far, so good.

You can follow Keiko's progress on the Internet. His official home page address is www.aquarium.org/keiko/index.htm.

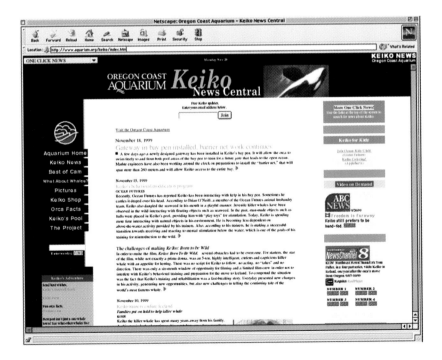

CHƏPTER 7

Orca Tales

The Ainu of Japan believe killer whales rule the deep sea. The Eskimos carve pictures of "blackfish" on their totem poles. They say within the orca is the soul of a man. The Haidu Indians think the killer whale is the world's most powerful being. And the Nootkan whalers of the Pacific Northwest say orcas are "one step above God."

Many cultures have myths and legends about orcas. Three follow.

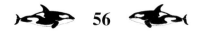

The Whale and the Eagle

Back in the time when the Great Raven made things, animals roamed Earth. They searched for a place to belong. Splendid in black and white feathers, Eagle soared high above. It was lonely in the sky. And Eagle cried into the wind, "Will I never find my place in the world?"

Beneath the sparkling ocean waves, Whale also traveled alone. She hoped for someone to share the journey. But her deep water world was an empty land.

One day, Eagle noticed a bird. It glided beneath him atop the water. Eager for company, he dipped lower.

Alas, it was only his shadow. Whale also noticed the dark spot and went to see what it was. She raised her head above the surf. Spying Eagle, she called, "Friend. Come closer. Let us speak together."

The two spent every day talking. They shared trinkets from their worlds, such as seashells, starfish, twigs, and blossoms. Soon they fell deeply in love. That only made them sadder. They lived in separate worlds.

One day, Eagle came at sunrise. Whale dove deep. Then she turned, rushed to the surface, and jumped for the sky. They mated in midair. Their children still wander the ocean today. They are orcas. They are black and white like their father Eagle. And they breach the water as their mother Whale did that day when two worlds joined in a love so strong that nothing could keep them apart.

THUNDERBiRD'S STORY

In the time before this time, it is said that animals had many of the same qualities as people. Once, a giant killer whale ate all the salmon in the ocean. Humans began to starve.

The chiefs gathered on the beach. "Please, Father Whale, go away."

The blackfish only mocked them, "Go away! Go away!"

Finally, a congress of the greatest chiefs assembled. After a time, a wild wind blew in from the sea. Lightning flashed. Thunder rumbled. The men felt the presence of an invisible spirit.

Its voice filled the air. "If I help you, what will you do for me?"

The chiefs promised to reproduce the spirit's likeness for all time. It would be a sign of their respect.

Satisfied, Thunderbird appeared. The enormous bird-god swooped toward the sea. His wings blocked the sun. Thunder rolled beneath them. Lightning flashed from his pointed talons as he snatched up the killer whale. The **raptor** spirit dropped the evil blackfish onto the land. There, it turned into a rocky mountain.

Native carvers have kept their word ever since.

The Tale of
Natsihlane

Many years ago, there lived a Tlinglit Indian woodsman named Natsihlane. He lived in the land of snow now known as southeastern Alaska. His country was rich with game—finned, furred, and feathered. Of all his tribesman, Natsihlane had the most skill. This made his brothers-in-law jealous. All, that is, except the youngest.

One day, while on a hunt, the brothers-in-law abandoned Natsihlane on a distant island. The youngest despaired as they paddled their canoes away. Natsihlane felt very sad. "Will I ever see my family again?" he cried.

That night, a seagull came and flew him to the home of the sea lions. Their chief put Natsihlane inside an inflated sea lion stomach and put it in the water. "Think hard about the beach near your village."

Natishlane did as instructed. And soon, he found himself home. Planning revenge on his brothers-in-law, he collected

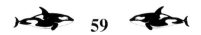

different pieces of wood and whittled blackfish from them. He tried spruce, red cedar, and hemlock. On each, he painted stripes of different colors. But no amount of singing or shouting would bring them alive.

Finally, Natsihlane carved fine yellow cedar into eight large and small blackfish. He painted each with a white band across the head and a white circle around the dorsal fin. Singing his most powerful songs, he commanded them to go. Soon, the bay filled with spray from their spouting and playing.

After some days, Natsihlane noticed his brothers-in-law canoeing far out to sea. "Go," he told the blackfish. "Destroy all but the youngest."

They swam out and around and around the canoes. The men and boats all disappeared. But two blackfish saved the youngest and carried him to shore.

Natsihlane called to them, "I made you to get revenge on my brothers-in-law, not to kill human beings. After this, you shall not harm people. But you will help them when they are in trouble. Now go."

And they swam out to sea. They were the first orcas in the world.

Glossary

assassin   killer; murderer

carnivore   flesh-eating animal

census   count of an entire population

dialect   regional variety of language distinguished by vocabulary, grammar, and pronunciation

dorsal   back or near the back

echolocation   process of locating distant or invisible objects by means of sound waves reflected back to the one sending the waves

evolve   to change over a very long period of time

ferry   boat that carries people and goods across a body of water

innovative   relating to doing something in a new way

instinct   inborn knowledge

knot   variable unit of speed used for sea and air navigation

marine   relating to the sea

matriarchal   relating to a family or group headed by a female

melon   rounded organ in the front of some whales' heads

migration   movement from one region to another for breeding or feeding purposes

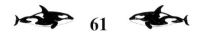

ogre	monster; hideous giant
pH	measure of acid and alkaline of a solution. Seven indicates neutral. Lower numbers indicate the acid, and higher numbers indicate the alkaline.
pinnipeds	suborder of aquatic, carnivorous mammals with all four limbs modified into flippers
plankton	tiny animal and plant life that floats or swims weakly in a body of water
pod	group of whales
porpoise	to roll over and over
predator	animal that hunts and eats other animals
raptor	bird of prey
reason	to think things out
rehabilitate	to get well
revenge	act of getting even
ruminant	relating to mammals that chew the cud and have a four-chambered stomach
snippets	tiny bits and pieces
species	class of individuals having common characteristics
unique	one of a kind
unison	together at the same time

Index